THE BANNED MAN

Shaun McCarthy

HIPPOPOTAMUS PRESS

ACKNOWLEDGEMENTS are due to the editors of the following magazines: *Bananas, Doors, Orbit, Ore, Poetry and Audience, Poetry Review, Present Tense, South West Review.*

The author gratefully acknowledges the financial assistance of South West Arts, who gave three awards towards the completion of this book.

The Hippopotamus Press gratefully acknowledges the financial assistance of the Arts Council of Great Britain.

First published 1984 by
HIPPOPOTAMUS PRESS
26 Cedar Road, Sutton, Surrey.

British Library Cataloguing in Publication Data
McCarthy, Shaun
The Banned man
I. Title
821'.914   PR6063.A163

ISBN 0-904179-31-1
ISBN 0-904179-32-X Pbk

*Twenty-five copies of this edition are
numbered and signed by the author*

Printed in Great Britain
by Skelton's Press Ltd., Wellingborough, Northants

Contents

FOR J. M.

I

JUST AS THEY DESCRIBED

Just as they described: steep descent,
a brook in the gutter, the sea a skyward mirror
tilted in the hedge. That white 'Atlantic'
on the cliff would be where they parked
the Alvis tourer: it's private now.
I pay to congest the narrow pier,
queue with a motorway at my heels:
they drove all day, without signposts,
on village green roads, from a blitzed city.

Boatmen usher you down to a slatted seat
on the 'Maid' or 'Belle', the worn engines thud;
the cliff path switchbacks airily
to that famous crag set to topple
through blue, endless afternoon sky.
And yet it's all changed; their Brownie's
narrow view would be well-aimed
to enclose the same scene. Inflatables
tug at bright cords, water-skiers swerve at rocks.

It's all too much like anywhere else;
like everywhere is. Distributors' vans
sway along minor roads to bring
the new ice cream, pandemic game,
the radio's songs . . . . I try to recall
an era I never knew; the brightness dims
for a moment but nothing fits. Jostled, I fling
borrowed guides onto the backseat, turn
uphill to join the Holiday Route.

TWO SHORT FILMS

Black and white, a dancer's skirt
of contrasting panels fills like a sail.
A cartoon skirt with no legs inside
partnered by a flap-armed shirt
who swoons like an Arab to Mecca,
rises, stalks a flamenco pose.

Animate washing, they tumble, kites in a tangle –
Two nudes, tanned and panting, step out of the scribble.

Black and white, a dancer's fans
slip rehearsed glimpses of hip and thigh,
beltless, cordless, barely in rhythm
as if the dancer were treading water,
while the hovering wings tremble
and stroke, enfold her luxuriously.

Finale, both fans cover her frontways, quivering –
While they are still falling she vanishes, giggling.

ON HEMBURY FORT

I'm filming shadows on Hembury Fort;
clouds mass beyong sloping woods,
their shapes flow smoothly over the banks
like armies advancing at walking pace.
The quiet hillside is slipping back
to its old contour, root and badger
breach what invaders could not.

I'm searching round the perimeter ditch
for potent signs, a sliced bough
as ritual club, between two flints
a coin burred to a spent gleam
spins and lands mint in my palm.
The ramparts steepen, bushes move,
pits smoke in the hide-strung trees,
sacking and cloaks stir in the breeze.

I'm checking the view with a parchment map:
here a bondsman ploughs a hill
steep as a wheel rim, a church peeps
from a valley narrow as cleavage.
Some huts are drawn by a reedy stream,
some more, like stooks, are ringed by a dyke,
their wealth portrayed by crooked folds.

I'm handing over the flap of hide;
the wind carries it off the bank,
a runner departs down through the woods
I follow him with my whirring lens
and pick out new features; silos, grey panes
of reservoirs, the smudge of towns.
They lie like tracings over my map's bounds:
on Hembury Fort I'm sure of my ground.

TRAVELLERS' TALES

It's curious how lives cross:
like my own and others made palpable
to me through words. But it appears
I'm always a little late or
too young to have paid the native price:
the old quarter's on every itinerary,
historic silhouettes spiked with antennae . . .
The shadow of a figure writing fades.

An elysian sonnet, an improbable phrase;
and a man booked in to a remote bay
where 'the timeless casting of fishermen
is staged against sheer beauty.'
He awoke, adrift in his first night,
as refrigerated lorries revved
and fumed beneath his balcony –
It's curious how lives cross.

The shadow of a figure writing fades;
the guide admits no counter-witness
to wonders invented, ghosts concocted,
confided straight-faced
by fierce mouthed locals with eyes on the present
to guileless strangers with eyes for the past.
What endures of a halcyon noon? Haze?
An elysian sonnet, an improbable phrase.

THE AGENT EXPLAINED

The agent explained
how the whiteboard elevation
wiped clean, veneered with plastic;
and I turned from my double image
in the insulating glass to watch

the solemn boy in a tracksuit bouncing
a bright football carefully.
Steep drives and low white fences
do not throw back a winning kick.

The climbing road ends at a gate
closed upon a rescued clump of oaks
from which the descending estate is named,
the chimneyless, green roofed houses
shed like cartons from a crashed load;

beyond thin hedges the wired bales
of crisp red bricks are hauled towards
another grove, or parkless lodge,
or spattered culvert due to be piped,

their names retained as if continuity
with things condemned might reassure,
any more than the street of slums that opens
on to cinder wastes, named Prospect Way.

VOICE ON THE WATER

VOICE ON THE WATER

1. *Giving Voice*

'I cannot go forward
do not want to go back.
Trees by the roadside
sigh as I pass them
like augers disputing
they wave ragged arms,
foliage seethes
sap boils in rage.
Trick wind blows up
at an unheard whistle
but turns no sail
carries no seed.

I will go anywhere
given a sign,
a gesture, or even
some clue in code . . . .
But nothing comes
I am left here
a blind man groping
neither forward nor back,
a rich man
with a waiting carriage
and four dead horses
between the shafts.

B. S. Johnson
took to a trawler:
sick in his bunk

rocked over shoals
he sifted his past
examining all
the bones that stuck
in his sieve, came home
a stronger man
but hopeless sailor.
The monsters and small fry
were sorted from his catch.'

    'Who is this
    who writes these lines?
    Who is this, whose key still fits,
    coming back after all these years,

    opening doors, asking for more light,
    as though nothing between us has changed,
    as though he has every right to be here?

    He has none!
    This shadow world
    is not his, he trespasses
    on things he discarded, I

    who dwell on detritus have heard the lies
    the deceits he's spread since leaving here,
    falsehoods thin-woven to win approval –

    I am damned
    for my stubborn truth!
    But this doppel-gänger's twin,
    unwelcome prodigal, comes

    to a house long razed. Though I take him in
    he shuns his true face, a louring cloud
    that looms straight through four walls of sky.'

'I dread the cadaverous eyes
of the moonlit past . . . .

Sometimes into my own
a lunar crescent seeps,
sometimes it grows gibbous . . . .

But until I face that gaze
I cannot warm
to the noon sun.

For that I live
lover and loved
without self-knowledge
without confirmation,
and that I prosper
or trivially lose is true,

but a void within me
is slowly expanding,
a tower
of twenty four years
standing on sand
slipping grain by grain . . . .

I cannot for long believe
principles I barely hold,
they brand me a chameleon, whose tones
are camouflage
or pure effect.'

2. *Schooldays and Fireworks*

('I remember the icy playground slide
down which I slipped to manhood . . . .')

In those days there were only extremes
flaming Junes or bleak Novembers:
class-room dog-days of lassitude
motes rising in a milky stench,
or winter dusks, jogging numb
from football, and the agony
of thawing fingers frozen mid-field.

Through these extremes I wove a path
that a single thread of silk would trace
between the wefts of uniform serge,
fought my way from the shaken fence
to the playground's whirling hub, then turned
self-consciously tallest and walked away
through a juvenile throng of strangers at bay.

What I hated most was the playing field,
I developed neither the skill to win
nor that diplomatic gamesmanship
whose virtues were tooled on unreachable shields,
but my team-mates, who were full of both
are still there, though married and disbanded,
keeping their noses clean, their eyes
on the ball, far out on some stoney pitch
on the blighted playing fields of England.

* * *

Schoolboy swinging an outsize briefcase
hurries raggedly home at dusk.
From his room he scans autumnal gardens
where acrid wisps may be the start

of sparks and flares set to swirl
above scorched walls into the sky
we notice only twice a year:
at Christmas new stars shoot like sleighs

and tonight, above school, bad marks and games,
a whoop of fire spills from a rocket's tail.

Remember, remember . . . .
Golden Rain, Dragon's Tooth and sulpherous Etna
gaudy cones leaking fine grey dust,
fewer each year, taken to heart

the close-ups of faces basted with blood.
That old toy shop has been pulled down,
there the glass topped trays were stacked
with charges enough for a rainbow blitz.
But the new retail chain does not advertise
afraid of inviting the moral blame
for Casualty's night-book of pain.

And yet each year I watch the sky
for shooting stars, standing at dusk
by the uncurtained window, faintly aware
of a moth I have attracted in
whirring around inside the lamp
its papery wings charred by the bulb.

With cupped hands I could set it free
from its prison of light, but then I might miss
some dazzling rocket just being lit,
so I stare fixedly into the gloom
the frantic tattoo a shadow in the room.

Then the first shrieking plume flies up
consumes itself, falls as a cinder –
and I am appalled by a sudden silence.

Night thickens. The last firework
lands with a rattle. Stars recapture
the sky's luminosity. Under the trees
darkness is total. Voices fade . . . .

3. *Dream and Waking*

Sometimes I dream I am in a pub
buying drinks for my friends.

Beside me a girl sits at the bar,
she is on her own

and is pretty and because I am standing up
I can see down her dress.

I buy her a drink in a nonchalant way:
my friends have disappeared.

She knows that my dream-self is racing ahead,
she plays my desires

her look acquiescent. The way she gets up
I know it is decided.

* * *

A secret his youth demanded but could not keep
closed like a flower he could not unfold
though nightly he straddled it in his sleep.

But far from dreams he coarsened his voice to break
in tune with cronies equally sham:
all of them nursing the same dull ache.

At claimed prowess he smiled, able to plot
thoughts like his own, the oscillation
from fear of acting, to shame of not.

Until in some mundane room his dreams came clear
a seemingly latent impulsion seeped
like gas in a volatile atmosphere.

Igniting his blank resolve, so long at bay,
reality took her face, took him up
like a wave lifting him where they lay:

and it seemed he'd lived up to then submerged, unaware
of the sun on the water to which he now rose
supine through fathoms of filtering jade,

to the calm surface, to utter rest.

* * *

If I colour the truth of my early loves
then compromise with your own half-lies,
marshall my vapid cast in masks
drawn from memory, torpid eyes
ill-fit rigid sockets, mad to re-live
you offer no love to soften their visor's clasps.

Productions change but the play's perennial;
whoever's the actor, his speeches are master.

I progress like a counter in a game
I tire of 'Passing Go', through rules I know
too much of other peoples' lives:
action and paradigm ramify, flow
with seasonal flux, brave new world
is a freak condition, an icing of sudden snow.

My footprints fall in with others impressed
in the frozen mud, marched under drifts.

And deeper down, under hollow floors
is the iron hoop where manacles hung
in a vaulted cell where they bricked-up time.
Here is the niche where inquistors wrung
confessions with tongs, deeper still
are ruins of earlier cells and dens of crime.

We live on a surface brittle as ice
the flow undermines, but frost binds the cracks.

4. *Voice on the Water*

To find my voice
in the written word
the tense a bridge
fluid as water
past and present
spanned in one stanza
shaping the next.

The bubbles in a drawn tube
rise precisely
like ants in line,
tongues of water in a sump
plait together
bearing away
grass-stems on their lizard backs.

The recommencement after rain!
Footfalls of people leaving shelter
rhythm of the gutter's dripping,
butts evenly brimming.

Dry at my desk
diverting the stream
this way and that
a hopeless task
I try to phrase
memories in water,
draw understanding

from the cataract's voice.

* * *

'An author as ghost of his own infancy
recounts distant childhood in best-selling form,
spanning the years his accomplished pen
demeans to anecdote outgrown fear.

But here's a writer far too young
even to claim the title with grace,
scars on his knees have barely healed,
so why does he work this theme like a sore?'

Because I have no better past
and am lodged in an eternal present
like Santayana's amnesic man,
without perspective all's repetition –

no promise, but a perpetual relapse
into what has gone before,
an aphyllous future, unending autumn
gathering leaves that were never green.

Work drafted. Now cicatrized skin
must be split back. Slack nerves unpicked
will not connect. Like gutting fish
the pain is detached. Nothing bleeds . . . .

I dive deep
as a fish descends
to phosphorescent
sea-floor dunes.
The sonorous volume of memories
squeezes the drum in my head.

Down here, no wrecks to shelter in
no smuggled lighter, rust inscribed

propped in a basket of polished ribs,
there is only impenetrable depth
shelving away, inexplicable swirls
and the silent bloodless predators
gliding implacably over the sand:
spawned into limbo, unevolved
their airless cells numbed to buoy up
the teeming life of the warm sunlit world.

5. *The Sea Monster*

Trawled up by an unlucky net
to a world it had not dreamed existed
the fish collapsed, dead on landing,
air like a bell had exploded it.

Fishermen shrank from the fo'c'sle hatch
on which it sprawled, fearing revenge
in its saucer eye and predatory fin.

Someone recalled the shark that swam
tirelessly round its tank for weeks
though its brain had been ripped out:
but this fish-thing was something else.

It was as if a unicorn
had been mistaken for a deer and shot,
the crew were frightened because they had killed
something unique, something watched over –
they feared a reprisal, their nets had taken
a precious son from the sea-god's lap.

* * *

What's all this about fish?

Cod on the slab ooze brine like blood
my dreams give them life, but grilled
they leave a skeleton the cartoon cat
pursues through his comic adventures.

I'm no fisherman, I loathe the sport,
much less a fish, having ears not gills –

but words take over and though I fight
against the pen to hold my theme
I succumb like a medium entranced
a living receiver/decoder, no more,
a mechanical hand, without volition
commandeering differently headed sheets
for transcripts from the vociferous dead.

Now a lifeless coelocanth
flops onto the page!
Am I to pity its tragic death,
flayed by sun and air?

'What about me?' The hysterical voice
issues from the dummy's wooden mouth.

My life is stacked away in crates,
enticing components litter the floor,
but there's something lacking, something of me
trapped in my past for the poem to free –

But without this shadowy animus
I cannot write the poem!

'What about me?' The square, hinged mouth
claps open and shut but can say no more.

The sea fades. Only a dream
an image at best. A child is running
up through the surf. With every step
he grows by a year. Voices rise . . . .

6. *Church Street*

We all enjoy
going home.
At home we can see
successive past selves
like cinema stills,
lambent projections.
I imagine a footage
of children, all me,
posed by the door
where I used to chalk
my height each birthday.
There they stand
one year apart,
each with a breathless
party grin.

I watched the doors of that old house
defaced with slogans of teams and pacts
thrown like huge leaves onto the blaze
piled up to gut the swollen terrace
so a new road could go through.

I cried when only the walls were left
revealing the paper I'd chosen myself,
galleons on repetitious seas,
and the crumbled fireplace hanging in space.

They knocked out our house
like a hollow tooth,
then broke the jaw.
The hidden rooms
and double turns
suddenly gaped
to the cleared view
of three lanes North,
three South, marked out
with orange tapes
dissecting the courses
of walled-in lives,
as though two plans
were overlaid
each transparent,

one, in blueprint, an impression, expansive,
the other, a jumble of back to backs
a cellular pattern of cramped partitions
mean conversions, blank abutments.

So they knocked out our teeth, and the street disappeared
its life dispersed towards better things –
slum propinquity held no-one in sway.
Cats and roseplants were left to go wild

and the old were put into care.

* * *

But even if
I could go back
to stand against
that old yard door
and add one last
impressive mark
to the scale of heights,
what would it prove?
Some coming of age?
But feet and inches
are surmountable now,
and five foot nine
is no Grenadier
except to a little boy
playing at soldiers.

Nostalgia I find is cheap,
it loves at safe distance
things irredeemable.
Stooping to sit at the old school desk
or driving slowly past a house

you once called home
is like putting flowers
on an empty grave:
no sadness there
but indulgent grief.

Love cannot die
and it alone
fired and gave magic to this child,
defined his world with its vigilance:

love cannot die
through age alone,
it's his only home, his bed is kept made,
an ear half-cocked for his key in the door.

7. *Storm*

My jars of wine ferment by the fire,
one lamp is enough
for my wife and I.
Outside a neighbour's guests depart,
voices harangue the squalling rain,
an engine is revved too hard.

Our first floor room commands the dark road
from its jutting bay I glance down
as an Admiral might through windows set
high in his galleon's corbelled stern.

My skin is cold about me tonight
I fill it like clay fills a mould,
I trespass in my bed, this house
my home, feels like a derelict shelter.

But on stormy nights like this remember
it's worse on the coast, the seagulls have flown
this far upstream to sit it out,
on my roof they find where the heat seeps through.

Though gales wrench pilings from the mud,
untie sailors' knots, steal the soil
from the sleeping root, defy the barrage
that buffets your head, gusts that writhe
like maddened dogs, see through the sky's crack

if any omnipotent hand is raised
to draw the inchoate world to heel,
calming the horses that shy on the brink,
rocking sea and sky like a baby
so the open boat riding the flood
rocks gently as a cradle.

Keep your faith!
I fill sandbags
my dull ballast
of empiric reason –

something to build on.

Dawn gathers. The pylons are down
but lamps suffice to return to homes
the flood has vacated. I force the door
to my waterlogged mind. Strange river-smells . . . .

Protean light throws shapes on water
hatches the reflection of a man
who walks in the air
but has stepped from a vacuum beyond –

like a Catholic steps from confession.

He enters on the brink of a river in spate
or stares at his slithering image towed
from the rail of a North Sea trawler . . . .

'But shadows cast my design
make an I-Ching of my past
a stick for each dead year.'

      'And what is the answer they give?'

'Nothing but what I knew before
which is enough for a little belief
but being an occidental man
I would have preferred a blinding flash.'

* * *

In the past there is nothing
but claims worked out,
what matters lives on
and what lives on
is a pebble in a pan,
a malleable ore.

I am malleable, my flesh
masses over my bones
like cloud that gathers round crags.

Right and wrong
one heart, one choice,
are concepts that cannot prescribe nor prejudge:
the echoes rebound but can voice no more
than late opinions on things gone before.

Right or wrong
bleak heart, cruel choice,
these verdicts are fake to a world not yet born:
they damn us for what we are or have been
but not for what we dream of becoming,

and though they cluster at my heels they cannot guide
this pioneer man crossing the unmapped divide.

II

THE PEARL DIVER

Shoals break at his plunge
lilac, pink and yellow fins
erect, concealed spines.

A turtle rises
the diver flexes downwards
each to precious eggs.

He dips like a kite
above sand concealing wealth
and is tugged upwards.

Quiet of a garden
gentle prismatic currents
pale legs climbing out.

FAMILIAR BANDAGES

A little boy stood before the glass,
the mummy towered over him, stiff as a plank.
The boy mistook the smell of polish
for sweet gum seeping through the cloth.
When people passed the cabinet
the mummy stirred.

To me Egyptology's taboo, those photos taken
by cameras thrust through the fissured wall, pure terror.
Exhibition panache could not restrain
such bandaged strength, warmed by the lights.
Practical jokers surgically wrapped
and rigid mock a potent curse.

On a foggy night near Russell Square
a padding figure, muffled, enormous,
lurched before me and heaved apart
the iron gates of a mansion block.
I heard him joke with the porter,
he smiled at me.

But a word stirs the dusty lungs like puffing lizards:
the lid is askew, a gaselier dashed; Herr Professor
stumbles in terror round the locked museum.
My fate is worse, I am trussed
by familiar bandages, powerless, hearing
the cursed stone inching down the shaft.

THE LOCK

Friends not lovers,
chance implications
somehow fewer,
leaning together from a stone bridge
to see how the sleeping water lay
in the scummed, deep-chambered lock.

It frightened you
but you wanted me to see.

Tonight there's a lot
of water between us,
furrowed by liners
ceaselessly passing, driven on music;
couples embrace at the rails, their doubles,
ploughed by the wake, dissolve.

We lie with our lovers
in curtained rooms, steadied on gimbals:

but I, at least,
in the balanced calm
remember a sudden, less perfect ease,
the light brush of two faces reflected
on the bridge's inverted crest
deep in unmoving water.

ON HOW TO CHOOSE A STONE

First select a target and decide
whether the aim is to hurt or not;
stones like boomerangs can come back:

loose pebbles tossed into a thicket
confuse a sheriff's posse;
under city walls on the desert's edge
among camps and middens are strewn
the jagged flints picked for ritual stoning.
Half-bricks and cobblestones
are best for riots. Insurgents burst
through cordons onto spacious malls
to pelt those who guard official windows.

The beach is a range for games with stones:
flakes for skimming, smooth dodo eggs
for depth charging pools, slick implosions.
The only target is the skinless sea
and she is a contemptous queen,
mother of all the hive of stones.

Finally, for the adventurous,
are boulders, precariously lodged
above strategic passes. Spadework
round the base and a lever behind
tumbles an avalanche, enough
to crush a convoy
or scatter a marauding band.

Never tie messages to stones;
they carry their own, no matter
what you mean by throwing them.

WHEN WORDS ESCAPED....

When words escaped the press to steer my course
I drifted on slack water, unalarmed,
ghosting their rhythm, muted iambics
like my heartbeat, the pattern that life

itself was grounded on, and since I lived
then lines I sought, though yet unmarshalled
would in due course be energised;
as lines that hum the advance of awaited trains.

'Awaiting ideas,' I'd say to friends
curious why my desk was clear
of drafts and grand designs. Glossing the calm
I misread the signal's remotely triggered signs.

Was there some remote shift of favour
a tide that one bright noon ebbs out
and never returns for cargoes on blistering piers:
or did I return to see only wrecks and sand?

The banned man, archivist of horrors, folds his cuttings
into poacher's pockets; proof that he was the one who
was there
on the running board beside the toppled Gothic eagle.
That coat, semblance of cavalry uniform, hangs round
him still.
Attempts to confirm his past dissolve into
embellishments;
a solitary man, his silence swells a tribe of versions
barred by draconic laws, not by landlords' threats.
He sleeps in arcades, in a nest of tin and sacking
on derelict ground surrounded by spacious houses
where the curtains are left undrawn after dinner
and conversation turns like a delicate mobile
to the tree's raw scraping outside, and the banned man.

The banned man never asks nor thanks, but explains
his need.
He knows we like to know little. He is writing the epic of
his life
on toilet rolls donated by attendants.
He writes in his native Polish (or Hungarian, Czech,
Armenian.)
Trams lurch shattering through its pages, a coshed
motorman
is flung to the cobbles at the check-point. It tells also of
the prisoner
who vanished from the night train, of the black figure
who rises from unhallowed ground like candle smoke
and frightens children yet is their friend;
of the slain monster, the pit of wire and corpses

and of the one who survived: exile, spymaster,
excommunicant, fool. The bomb thrower, the banned
man.

    (All this, of course, is my device
    to cut a flag from a tattered coat,
    the sum no more than a score at dice –
    'Banned man,' clubbed cry stuck in my throat.)

A REPLY TO KEATS'
'TO ONE WHO HAS BEEN LONG IN CITY PENT'

To one who has been long enclosed by fields,
deterred by gates wired shut and seeded land,
these streets excite dulled senses – each has scanned
and, dazed by choice, knows banishment repealed.
The clouds seem to our moods more free to yield
from public vantage points more close to hand,
and later serried lights, musically fanned,
dispel the gloom where night would have us sealed.
Pleasure and commerce press you to delay
your homeward steps, then the comfortable pace
of strollers at the liquid rim of day
divert you to the river's twilight space:
a reach not tranquil, but where tenebrae
rebuilds its gleam; brightens the tearful face.

His Lordship is in the library
trying not to have to think;
amiable bumbler, he gazes disfocused at memoirs.
At the Grange someone or something threatens;
we don't know who or what, but hope
the mystery will grow into a spell
and not, in being too soon solved,
become mere crime:

perhaps Her Ladyship is concealing notes,
or her mad son may have slipped away
from his remote wing; kitchen girls tremble,
a parang is missing from the study wall. Or perhaps
a sinister priest, looking oddly like
Sir —— (black sheep), has arrived in the village:

lanterns glow in the ruined dovecote,
at 'The Bull' bovine suspicion prevails.

A train chuffs up the valley, a taxi
arrives on set, bringing the gentleman-detective.
After dinner the dowager untangles
a Smith and Wesson from her bag, screams
tumble the back stairs, a poker is found in the laurel –

In the study survivors assemble
tension and logic mount
and the villain is accused with the jab of a pipe stem.
He shoots, himself or at someone else,
and ends up on the rug, a chalk figure.

The twitter of birds and domestics is brought up;
there's a romance to conclude, the inheritance to settle –

But you and I, seeing order restored
exit with the villain; without him the reel
shrinks towards blankness, platitudes, satisfied expressions;
the cheerful, awful fanfare and lights up.

opens with a burst of slang,
a Thompson's full clip sprayed.
A long car gets is broadside
and goes down on its rims like a horse to its knees.
'FOR RENT' glows through slatted blinds,
the girl breathes smoke and lets a strap slip down.

The story's always halfway through
everyone owes something, chews a grudge;
parole day nears, a caller has valuable photos.
The busy cameras ride downtown
like a newsteam tipped on imminent disaster.

The hero is hired by the day
and is often hit on the head;

he is bourbon gruff, knows observant barmen
and hookers always on a night off.
He shadows intuitions, hunches after hunches
through a labyrinth of hotels, morgues, front seats
of oversprung cars, pools of light
in rifled offices of frosted glass.

Confronting the villain presages a battle;
the cops arrive late and howling to verify scores.
The shamus is warned again that all this shot-up glass
is thin ice, spotted with citizens' blood;

but the D.A. gives him one more break
though woken by 'phone. Dawn bleeds tired faces.

The hero returns the evidence
to the heiress supine on her pool –
Her thanks are cool,
she saves her kindest gaze
(the one, well rehearsed, where she slips dark glasses down)
for his sleek sedan as it leaves her lonely.

From: IN MOTION

VASCO BALBOA AND THE WHEEL

A Shakespearian rogue
clumsy behind drapes
in the princess's chamber.
A banter-monger
and ready blade, more keen
to slice belts and send pants falling
than press to heart the point.

For him fortune's wheel revolved
to a fairground tune. He leapt
at the jingled purse into roistering crowds:
westward first to San Domingo
avoiding scandal, then on again,
smuggled this time past creditors
scouring the wharves, to Darien;

and bouncing down the gangplank there
lucky Vasco ducks the crossfire
of insurrection and scoops the governorship.
In similar vein he embarks,
like an equitorial alpinist,
to peek at the nameless ocean
on the world's undiscovered rim.

This sanguine swashbuckler
fleshes no historical claim,
but every schoolboy has seen
'From a Peak in Darien' –
The amazed musketeer pointing
over tree tops to a slip of blue,
a captain mouthing its future name,

and ebullient Balboa, a head above both,
looking as though he knew all along.

But hard to keep faith
with sanguine hope when home
must be fled before morning,
when cultivation wilts under jungle's thrall
and territories imperiously gained
are dispensed to interlopers.

His feet were more firmly in the earth
than his head was in the air, in his life
how often accomplishment sank to dissolution.

A young forty two, awaiting execution
at Santa Maria on the orders
of scheming in-laws, perhaps
he looked as he did that day
on the mountain: as though
he'd known this all along.

PIZZARO ON GALLO

He drew a line, there and then,
there in the sand.
                    Those who were with him
crossed over, the rest were sent back,
like frightened or erring children.
                              Thirteen
voted by a single pace to press ahead
when Ruiz returned.
                    (He, shipless in Panama,
was canvassing and button-holing
from palace to water-front
and all degrees between
for civic money and a command
to rescue the men on Gallo.)
                              Meanwhile
we thirteen complained evenly;
Pizzaro stalked the shore for a sight of his fleet.

The island water was spare and brackish,
tempers welled at its mean level.

Eventually Ruiz came, skippering a pitiful tub;
all he could beg.
                    From this dismissal
we embarked on the conquest
of empires, the purgation
of barbarous polyidolatries.
                              At Tumbez
we whored and traded for intelligence,
then returned to Panama for royal consent.

We were sober in the drinking dens;
those who had rooted on trodden sand
called for us to recount
our holidays on Gallo.
                           But we were patient,
loyal to absent Pizzaro,
certain in our sourness
that dour pessimism
is a great and dependable strength.

We began, that spring,
with Juana's blessing, 1532,
our royal hunt for the sun.

CORTEZ AT TENOCHTITLAN

My Victorian encyclopaedia
praises Cortez, a sort of Catholic Caesar
'His character constructed on historic lines.'

A man who burned alive
seventeen princes, while
betrayed and chained Montezuma
was forced to watch
the serial horror
of each vassel's agony.

A man between Cort and Cortona
'Inspiring the tenderest affections.'

His brief reign no statues salute –
In public life there was no compassion,
no hand unclenched save in lust.

La Noche Triste, 1st July, 1520

'Despised and mortal at last!
I heaped faggots round their two
most hideous idols, igniting them
on the high terrace in full view.
Spears wavered, headgear rocked,
but ranks held their disposition.

Midnight, at the year's dead centre,
we began our retreat.
Montezuma, labile old fool,
still weeping from his stoning,
we gutted and dumped in the lake.

Our path was the bare causeway,
over spans our besiegers had removed.
We built a pontoon to drag along
to bear our ordnance and horse.

A dismal failure!
All foundered at the second crossing;
breastplate and cabasset
weighed face down in bristling foam.
Bears in a pit; a rout.

Club wielding mobs hammered the crawling
to pulp. One by one my walking wounded
straggled off the landward end
to be ambushed at Otumba.'

Thus a sanguine man,
upright bearer of arms.
When he in turn
besieged the city
the Indians fear
of bloody reparations
left fifty thousand dead,
the island citadel razed.

His brief reign savage friars abetted –
In public life there was no compassion,
no hand unclenched save in lust.

His old age was bitterness,
a sinking from Hera to Aidoneus;
blood soured with base black bile.

This, my anonymous contributor concludes
was a man whose life
resembled 'A romantic fable . . . .'

THE SWEATING PRIESTS

The sweating priests draw close their circle:
martyrologists, reverers of cadavers,
flayers, cowled inquisitors.

Water their god's interpreter,
but they spoke fire, followed
the sprinkled blessing with brazier
and branding tongs; for heretics
no word but breath of flames.

Baptism preceded sentence; they vowed
that certainly god would rather hoard
souls in heaven than steer peace on earth.

In Darien a whore displayed
a golden sun between scarred breasts;
plunder dispensed by her master, a cleric.

They sailed into the sun from the bellies
of stale churches, its fire
cicatrized their compassion.

May the rockets poised for new planets
bear nothing cruciform.

AGUIRRE, THE WRATH OF GOD
(W. Germany, 1972, 95 mins, colour.)

Things fall apart;
the expedition is divided.
Some have constructed rafts
on a flood sliding nowhere.

The director broods;
Kinski threatens to scrap his contract,
a costume girl pines for her lover in Hamburg;
everyone spends days stumbling over roots.

But such vegetation!
That magnificent opening scene,
long zoom in to the shambling line
of musketeers, porters, the infanta
in a veiled sedan swaying down
the vertigious Andean pass
into oblivion.

Their striken leader is condemned
by the upstart Aguirre, already demented;
haunted by grimacing monkeys, inspired
by priests and their seeds of boyhood terror.

Everyone despairs. It rains for days.
The schedule pulps to a jungle leaf,
flight cases are fumbled into the mud.
At Lima vital lenses
lie impounded, lacking papers
no-one knew were needed.

Aguirre sinks into doomed empires,
bent on exacting biblical wrath
on naked sinners who flee like whispers
among tuberous roots of soft poison,
leaving feather signs, gore on stakes,
votive silences, hollow masks . . . .

Each can of film sent back to Europe
is as precious to the crew
as gold was to Aguirre's men.

WATER

They are one-voiced in the gloom, this shuffling hoard,
last of the day-trips to tour sequestered galleries,
routed on threadbare runners once round the library
at arm's length from furniture. A tasselled cord
is the last prerogative of tongueless lords.
Gold thread in the weave of dusty livery
sheds motes that swim like fish in a tropical sea.
I dive in this sunken saloon, hunting reward.

Few words were written: estate books, occasional contracts,
the meagre account of four centuries occupancy:
a library enlarged by the yard, memoirs commissioned.
My words are spills of oil on busy sea,
shimmering coils, swept into prisms of fission
or viscid scum, a veil to shoaling literacy.

AIR

A faithless wishing of a wish unfathomed; the lift
we gave from services to campus said the heater
blew too hot. You fumbled the familiar shift
for fear of brushing her leg. Not cold but slower
blood than hers, you joked. Cocooned for an hour
we half-reclined in the dashboard's glow, adrift
in our hitch-hikers' yarns, threadbare florid power,
our student days; her parents' too, that rift
is mundane and absolute. She scanned my books
for the reading, dealt by each bend across the rear seat
and declaimed what I professed: the need to read.
Each generation suspects what it succeeds,
these rhymes, like my blood, are fetters to her beat.
My choler is mute at your teacher's forebearing look.

THE PASSING OF THE NAME

Exit the last title;
two sticks to the opaque interior
of a rest home's ambulance.
Never a backward look.

A local agent arranged the sale
to offset duties: first contents,
(the few good pieces sent to London)
the rest, Victorian suites and mouldering beds,
knocked down on site. By afternoon
hired vans had ploughed the carriage drive
to mud, the furniture into the sad stock
of draughty sales-rooms across the county.

That night vandals fired the house;
kids playing families or bivouaced tramps
ignited unsold lots with paraffin . . . .
In six hours it was gone.

Blackened gables too fractured by heat
to safely stand were bulldozed next day.
The village lamented its razing as they had
the branch line they never rode.
A city overspilling beyond the hill
purchased the rubble and sun-pricked cellars.
The blackened fountain was hauled away
to sprinkle a councillor's bungalow.

VOLUME 94
OF THE YALE SERIES
OF YOUNGER POETS